IMAGES
of America

ROUTE 66 IN KANSAS

The name of this lovely Route 66 traveler posing on the Kansas-Missouri state line is lost to history. She was about to travel 13 miles across the southeastern corner of Kansas through the towns of Galena, Riverton, and Baxter Springs before reaching Oklahoma. The box culvert on her left is still there, and the young lady will make another appearance at the end of our journey. (Authors' collection.)

On the Cover: The first alignment of Route 66 came down Willow Avenue, the north part of town known as "Gasoline Alley," and curved east on present-day Third Street to Military Avenue. A.T. Spencer's Shell station at Second Street and Willow Avenue was near where the railroad crossed Route 66 and hobos made their camp. Spencer kept a box of old clothing on hand to help those who rode the rails from town to town in search of work. (Baxter Springs Heritage Center and Museum.)

IMAGES
of America

ROUTE 66 IN KANSAS

Joe Sonderman and Cheryl Eichar Jett

ARCADIA PUBLISHING

ISBN 978-1-4671-1651-0

Published by Arcadia Publishing
Charleston, South Carolina

Printed in the United States of America

Library of Congress Control Number: 2015955297

For all general information, please contact Arcadia Publishing:
Telephone 843-853-2070
Fax 843-853-0044
E-mail sales@arcadiapublishing.com
For customer service and orders:
Toll-Free 1-888-313-2665

Visit us on the Internet at www.arcadiapublishing.com

Dedicated to Howard "Pappy" Litch and Joe Douffet

CONTENTS

ACKNOWLEDGMENTS

We are grateful for many interesting, enjoyable, and productive hours spent inside the Galena Mining and Historical Museum and the Baxter Springs Heritage Center. We owe special thanks to Fred Billingsley, Wilma Douffet, Linda Kennedy, and Steve Rider. Unless otherwise noted, all Galena and Riverton images are from the Galena Mining and Historical Museum, all Baxter Springs images are from the Baxter Springs Heritage Center and Museum, and all the other images are from the authors' collection.

INTRODUCTION

There are only 13.2 miles of Route 66 in Kansas, but it packs in as much history and adventure per mile as in any other state. The entire road is still there and can be driven without encountering a single mile of interstate.

Chief Black Dog of the Osage created the first improved road in the region, a trail connecting the villages and hunting grounds between present-day Baxter Springs and Arkansas City, Kansas. The trail was said to be wide enough for 30 horses to pass abreast. When an 1836 treaty forced the Cherokee Nation from the southeastern United States, all of what is now Cherokee County was designated as the Cherokee Neutral Lands, designed as a buffer between Missouri and the lands of the Osage.

The area was closed to white settlers, but the Reverend John Baxter came anyway in 1849. He built a trading post and inn at the springs on the Military Road connecting Fort Leavenworth with Fort Gibson in the Indian Territory. Baxter was killed by another illegal settler in a land dispute, but his name lived on.

During the Civil War, a small fort was established at Baxter Springs, and rebel guerillas led by William Quantrill attacked on October 6, 1863. They were driven back but ambushed a military wagon train and massacred over 100 men, mostly in cold blood, as they tried to surrender. In 1866, the Cherokee ceded the Neutral Lands back to the US government, and the area became part of the state of Kansas.

The cattlemen and cowboys came after the war. Since it was on the border with the Indian Territory, Baxter Springs found itself at the end of the Eastern Shawnee Trail. "The First Cowtown in Kansas" was a wild and practically lawless place until the cattle drives moved on. Then the town quieted down, and the springs became a resort destination.

A settlement called Short Creek had sprung up along the stream north of Baxter Springs. The Indians knew there was lead in the area, but most settlers did not think much of it until April 1876, when pure lead ore was found at the bottom of a farmer's well. A group of investors from Baxter Springs established a mining camp that they called Bonanza.

The boom came in February 1877. Two boys digging for worms discovered a major deposit of lead ore along Short Creek. Within months, 10,000 people descended on the area, and the Empire Town Company and the Galena Town Company had established rival townsites on opposite sides of the creek. The two towns were incorporated a day apart in June 1877.

"Red Hot Street," connecting Empire City and Galena, was known for gambling, prostitution, public drunkenness, and violent death. The competition between the towns heated up in 1877, when Empire City went so far as to erect a stockade to stop travel between the rivals. The townspeople of Galena burned it down, and Empire City became part of Galena in 1907.

Hard roads came early to Cherokee County because the mines demanded them. However, road building in Kansas was strictly a local concern until a state highway system was created in 1925. Businessmen funded the concrete highway from Galena to Riverton that opened in August 1922.

Baxter Springs and Riverton were linked by concrete by the spring of 1924, but due to a dispute over funding a railroad overpass, a gap remained between Galena and the state line.

Meanwhile, private associations were laying out their own highways. They gave them fancy names and were usually paid by towns and merchants to be on the route. Motorists were often routed miles out of their way on poorly maintained paths, and the trails often overlapped. Baxter Springs found itself on the Jefferson Highway, the Ozark Trail, and the Ozarks to Rockies Trail. The federal government finally stepped in to bring an end to the confusion.

When the federal system was being laid out in 1925, the hard roads already in place put Cherokee County on the proposed Chicago–to–Los Angeles highway. Cyrus Avery, Oklahoma highway commissioner, laid out the route that just happened to pass by his businesses in Tulsa.

The committee gave the primary east-west transcontinental routes numbers ending in 0. Even though this was not a transcontinental highway, Avery used his influence to win the number 60. Then Kentucky governor William J. Fields demanded no. 60 for a route across his state. A standoff ensued until Avery and his supporters noticed the catchy-sounding 66 was available.

The federal highway system became official on November 11, 1926, and Galena, Riverton, and Baxter Springs were officially on the "Main Street of America." The gap east of Galena was the final stretch of Route 66 in Kansas to be paved and was dedicated on August 11, 1927.

The fledgling 66 Highway Association partnered with promoter C.C. Pyle to stage a coast-to-coast footrace in 1928. The "Bunion Derby" made Route 66 front-page news. Guy Shields of Baxter Springs took part and passed through his hometown on April 19. His welcome was tempered somewhat because an injury had dropped him to 52nd place. Andy Payne, a half-Cherokee from the Route 66 town of Foyil, Oklahoma, won the $25,000 first prize.

During the Great Depression, Route 66 became John Steinbeck's "road of flight," portrayed in *The Grapes of Wrath.* The demand for lead had dropped sharply after World War I, and jobs were scarce. In 1935, violence swept Galena when miners tried to form a union. Gunfire rang out over Route 66. Gov. Alf Landon declared martial law and sent in the Kansas National Guard.

During the 1930s and 1940s, the population of Galena plummeted and many of the elaborate buildings on Main Street vanished. Baxter Springs fared a little better, as it was the financial capital of the mining district and the economy was more diversified. Although the town never allowed mining within the city limits, many mining executives lived there.

The post–World War II years were the Golden Age of Route 66, as the GIs returned home and America took to the road. Bobby Troup's "(Get Your Kicks on) Route 66" was a big hit, despite neglecting to mention Kansas. Roadside businesses thrived and Baxter Springs became a trucking center. Yet the speeds and sizes of vehicles on Route 66 increased and so did the toll from accidents. Big changes were coming.

Pres. Dwight Eisenhower saw roads as vital to national defense and road building as a way to stimulate the economy. His Interstate Highway Act of 1956 spelled doom for the Main Streets of America. Interstate 44 opened in 1961 and bypassed Kansas completely in order to connect to the Will Rogers Turnpike in Oklahoma, which had opened in 1957.

In June 1961, a bypass was completed around the Rainbow Curve and the Brush Creek Bridge north of Baxter Springs. In 1963, Route 66 was relocated in Galena from Main Street to Seventh Street, angling northward near Mineral Avenue to become a four-lane divided highway and connect with Missouri's new 66 just east of the state line.

Route 66 was officially decertified on June 27, 1985, but people from around the world still seek it out. The Kansas Historic Route 66 Association was founded in 1990 to preserve Route 66 heritage, and two years later, it led preservation efforts that saved the Brush Creek Bridge. In Galena, the "Four Women on the Route" started a revival by fixing up an old gas station and rescuing the old tow truck that inspired a beloved character in the movie *Cars.*

A journey along Route 66 in Kansas still appeals to those who think that the journey is just as important as the destination. It reconnects us with a sense of community, with an America that is not all franchised, sanitized, wired in, and in a hurry. That is not bad for 13 miles of roadway.

One

State Line

Route 66 passes through the heart of the Tri-State mining district, where rock shops were once a common sight. Residents placed some minerals for sale in the yard, perhaps along with some homemade baskets or furniture. Fletcher's Mineral Museum, four miles west of Joplin, added sweet cider and ice-cold sweet wine. (Courtesy of Steve Rider)

The tristate area is the home of the legendary "Spook Light." The bobbing ball of intense light appears on isolated back roads, four miles south of the intersection of the Missouri, Kansas, and Oklahoma state lines. Some think it is just refracting headlights from Route 66, several miles away, but locals say sightings have occurred since the 1860s. (Courtesy of Steve Rider.)

Tourists searching for the light could stop at the Spook Light Free Museum, or "Spooksville," a glorified shack on East 50 Road at State Line Road. It was originally built by photographer Arthur Posie Meadows, who did a brisk business in Spooklight postcards. Garland "Spooky" Middleton later took over and added a bar where he would regale the curious with stories of the Spooklight. The shack burned down sometime after he died in 1984.

Bars and honky-tonks lined Route 66 west of Joplin because Kansas was a dry state until 1948. Cherokee County, Kansas, did not allow the sale of liquor by the drink until 2012. Joe Mertz opened one of the more unusual bars near the line in 1950 at 1818 West Seventh Street. The Carnival Room at his Dutch's Top Hat boasted the only revolving bar in the state.

A small restaurant building was constructed at 2409 West Seventh Street about 1930 and was expanded several times over the years to become a landmark. Ken Browsky opened Ken's Bar here in 1951, and it became Dixie Lee's Dine and Dance in 1962. The building was the Route 66 Pit Stop in the 1990s but no longer stands today.

"Sunny" Jim Walters was a former professional baseball player who established the Little League park in Joplin named in his honor. He had a candy store on Main Street in Joplin and opened Sunny Jim's Ozark Candy Farm on Route 66 in 1954. In 1964, Jim and his wife moved to Loveland, Colorado, to open a new store. The building just before the turnoff to Old Route 66 became an auto auction service and is now abandoned.

Just past the remnants of Sunny Jim's, a sign reading "Old Route 66" marks the turnoff to the original route and the state line. It was once a lively stop for travelers and miners crossing the line to buy alcohol. The State Line Mercantile started out in 1925 as the small Gray and Archer gas station. The Paddoc family took over in 1979, and Norman "Wick" Anderson ran the business for over 20 years. Paddoc Liquors is still in business today.

Harry's Phillips 66 Super Station was located immediately to the east of the State Line Café and was operated by Charlie Haroldson for many years. Gas stations often clustered at the state line due to the differences in the gas tax from one state to the next. Harry's closed after the new highway opened, but the altered building still stands.

The State Line Café was the first stop for alcohol after leaving Kansas or the last before leaving Missouri. It was established in 1925 and operated by Fred Link and his wife, Marie. Neighbor Betty Barrett recalled being afraid to play around the café because relatives told her the gypsies that camped in the nearby woods would steal little children. The building became the Hogs and Hot Rods Saloon.

The liveliest spot on the state line was the Oasis Club, which opened on December 2, 1937. Located on the south side of the road, the Oasis had a dance floor that could hold 1,000 couples and was billed as the largest of its kind in the state. Harry Gray, Fred Wheeler, and Bill Archer's club attracted some of the biggest names in country music. It closed in the 1940s and eventually burned down.

Disaster was narrowly averted on April 18, 1952, when a fully loaded gas tanker careened off Highway 66 just east of the Missouri-Kansas line, smashed into the Grace Hatfield's T and J Café, and then hit a parked truck filled with explosives. The tanker driver and seven or eight people inside the café all got out safely.

The Hurst Auto Salvage Yard was located 100 feet east of the Kansas state line on Highway 66 and was operated by Harry Hurst from the 1930s into the 1950s. Hurst issued a series of postcards featuring scenes of ancient and rare automobiles rusting away in the salvage yard. These autos would bring high prices at auction today.

The souvenir stand immediately west of the state line could sell rugs and trinkets but nothing stronger than Coca-Cola. A Will Rogers Highway sign would be placed at the line in 1952 as part of a cross-country caravan to promote the movie *The Story of Will Rogers*. The marker is now located in Galena's Howard "Pappy" Litch Memorial Park.

The Historic Byway and Kansas US Route 66 signs greet modern Route 66 travelers at the Missouri-Kansas state line. All 13 miles, including older alignments, of the Kansas segment of historic Route 66 was designated as a Kansas Historic Byway in November 2011. The official designation placed the highway on the National Scenic Byways listing.

Two

GALENA

Hard roads came early to Cherokee County, because of the prosperity brought by the mines and the need to transport heavy equipment. There was also a handy source of paving material at hand, the massive piles of "chat," or mining waste. As early as 1904, crews—such as this one at Galena—had already begun paving roads with chat, which formed a solid concrete-like surface.

The Picher Lead Company, later Eagle-Picher, bought the Galena Manufacturing Company's lead smelter in 1912. The plant had started operation in 1902. The smelter became the largest employer in the area, processing lead, zinc, and cadmium ores and producing zinc oxide, zinc sulfide, manganese sulfate, manganese dioxide, and sulfuric acid.

Kansas governor Alf Landon ordered the National Guard to Galena and declared martial law in June 1935 after hundreds of striking miners blocked Route 66 in front of the Eagle-Picher smelter. Shots and rocks rained down on cars carrying strikebreakers from the Blue Card Union formed by the mining firms. Within a few weeks, most of the mines were on their regular production schedules and the union appeared broken. (Courtesy of Steve Rider.)

Violence erupted again on April 11, 1937, when hundreds of Blue Card men armed with pick handles marched on the Congress of Industrial Organizations (CIO) office in Galena. Nine people, including a child, were shot and wounded in the ensuing melee. The courts ruled that the company union was illegal, but it was a hollow victory for labor. Mechanization of the mines following World War II reduced the workforce, and the mines were eventually exhausted. (Courtesy of Library of Congress.)

This group of workers has gathered in the lunchroom at the Eagle-Picher smelter during the 1950s. From left to right are (first row) Clarence Nichols, Willie Elder, Earl Treadway, George Beets, Walter Porter, Willie Fritchey, Lester Sicrist, Alvin Baker, Harvey Williams, and Joe Inman; (second row) Emert Fichtner, Bill Gold, and Henry Nausley; (third row) Maurice Martin, Lee Fain, and Elza Alexander.

In 1954, a $4.6 million zinc-roasting and sulphuric acid plant was added to the Eagle-Picher facility. It became even more important to the area after the active mines mostly shifted to the Picher/Treece area. The plant closed in June 1980. The mining boom left behind 800 mine shafts and toxic levels of lead, cadmium, arsenic, mercury, chromium, and zinc in the soil and water. Almost nothing would grow on "Hell's Half Acre" along Route 66 near the old plant.

The US Geological Survey once named Galena as the most polluted city in Kansas. In 2006, Galena's image took a further beating when a collapsing mine shaft swallowed up a building housing the Green Parrot Bar. But the Environmental Protection Agency (EPA) and state and local governments combined efforts to fill shafts and clean up the soil and water. For the first time in almost a century, substantial vegetation is returning to Hell's Half Acre.

The last section of Route 66 in Kansas to be paved and a new railroad viaduct were dedicated with a bottle of precious pre–Volstead Act champagne on August 11, 1927. The original route had crossed to the north of the Missouri-Kansas-Texas (Katy or MKT) Railroad tracks in front of the smelter and crossed the St. Louis–San Francisco Railway (Frisco) tracks on Main Street. The viaduct and new route stayed south of the tracks and eliminated those dangerous crossings.

The Katy station opened in 1902 at the bottom of the hill on Main Street. After it closed in 1983, the Bill Hall family donated the landmark to the Galena Mining and Historical Museum Association, and it was moved next to the Municipal Complex on old Route 66. The museum was dedicated on June 2, 1984, and displays artifacts accumulated over decades by Pappy Litch.

Scott W. Palmer and his wife, Jennis, operated the scale shop located at 210 North Main Street in Galena near the old Empire City boundary. The shop sat just north of the boardinghouse that later became notorious as the alleged "Murder Bordello," visible at right. A right turn from Front Street onto Main Street here led to Empire City just to the north across Short Creek.

Frank Tryon's Grocery was in Empire City, the rival mining town on the other side of Short Creek. The rivalry turned ugly on July 25, 1877, when the Empire City council ordered a stockade erected along the southern city limits to prevent traffic between the towns. The mayor of Galena formed a posse of 50 men, and they attacked and burned the stockade at 4:00 a.m. on August 15, 1877. Only a few shots were fired, and no one was seriously hurt. Tryon's was later known as Faulkner's, and the building is still recognizable today.

Red Hot Street, situated between Galena and Empire City, was home to "innumerable haunts of dissipation and vice." One account says the "lewd and reckless were congregated at all hours, intoxicated by wine, lulled by the sweet strains of music, and lured on by the sirens' charms to deeds undreamed of." Empire City grew to a population of about 2,300, but it was long ago eclipsed by its rival to the south and became part of Galena in 1907.

When a deteriorating Victorian home at Front and Main Streets was being restored in 2012, the owners hinted it was haunted and might have been a brothel owned by "Galena's Bloody Madam," Ma Staffleback. The newspapers claimed the Staffleback family may have robbed and murdered up to 50 miners in the 1890s, but they were only convicted in one case. A mob burned down the real Staffleback cabin on the west end of town in 1897. (Galena's Murder Bordello.)

The alleged Staffleback connection has been disproven, but tourists can spend the night in the lavish style of an 1890s brothel at the restored "Murder Bordello." The owners offer tours and the occasional paranormal investigation. A group of artificial black crows arranged on a tree stump outside completes the madams-and-mayhem theme, as a group of crows is known as a murder.

The three-story Banks Hotel, located on the corner of Front and Main Streets, was the largest building in town and partly blocked the view of motorists making the left turn onto Main. In 1928, Galena officials launched a crackdown on drivers making "a racetrack" out of Highway 66 and ignoring the stop sign at the intersection. To the relief of drivers, the hotel was torn down in 1933. Emma Ellis and Charlie Land are shown here in the hotel lobby.

A gas station was built on the site after the Banks Hotel was torn down. Ray Routledge opened a Cities Service station here in 1948, and James Little took over in 1952. Garland Snooks and then Ernest Hayes later ran the station. At one time, the station sold Kan-O-Tex gasoline, a Kansas-based brand founded in 1909. The Anderson Pritchard Oil Company bought out Kan-O-Tex, and the stations were rebranded to APCO. (Courtesy of Melba Rigg.)

Calling themselves "Four Women on the Route," Renee Charles, Betty Courtney, Melba Rigg, and Judy Courtney restored the old, vacant Kan-O-Tex station and turned it into a visitors center in 2006. Their efforts started a Route 66 revival that has spread across Galena. Now known as Cars on the Route, the station features a diner, a selection of Route 66 souvenirs, and restored Kan-O-Tex gas pumps out front.

A rusty old 1951 International Series 170 tow truck parked next to the Kan-O-Tex station caught the eye of director John Lasseter and the crew of the Pixar film *Cars* as they traveled Route 66 seeking inspiration. The old truck became the basis for the character Tow Mater. A name change was necessary for legal reasons, and "Tow Tater" now greets kids at the station. Note the home that became the Murder Bordello across the street.

In 1896, Louis K. Moeller and Joseph H. Smith constructed a building at Front and Main Streets for their lumber supply business. Moeller had served as mayor of Galena in 1887–1888 and took over sole ownership in 1897. In 1930, the building became the Front Street Garage, operated by August Clarence Bradshaw and shown here in 1941 when it offered White Rose gasoline. The White Rose refinery was about 60 miles away in Coffeyville, Kansas.

August Clarence Bradshaw is pictured here waiting for customers at the Front Street Garage. He stopped selling gas during World War II and focused the business on selling new and recapped tires. Bradshaw died in March 1954, and the building later housed a satellite dish manufacturing and repair business until preservationist Ed Klein began restoration in 2014.

The lettering on the side of the old Front Street Garage remains from the days when it was the J.H. Smith Lumberyard. Ghost signs from the glory days of Galena also advertise the long-gone Palace Drug Store that was located at Sixth and Main Streets as well as three different brands of cigars: San Felice, Henry George, and Tom Moore.

Main Street in Galena was a busy place when the miners came to town to cash and spend their hard-earned paychecks on Saturdays. But nearly all of the structures in this 1896 photograph have been demolished, leaving behind vacant lots. The building that housed the Hub Furniture Store at the time still stands. It became Buck's Recreation, a bar and pool hall operated by Buck Dean.

Porter M. Clark ran a furniture and undertaking business in the Moore-Stice Block at 113–117 Main Street. He later moved to Fourth and Main Streets and also opened a branch in Baxter Springs. Clark founded the Hillcrest Cemetery and served as mayor in 1913–1914. There was no funeral when Clark died of heat prostration in July 1934. As per his instructions, a two-hour program of dance music was played at the cemetery by a 20-piece band from Webb City, Missouri.

Albert and Will Schmidt ran the Schmidt Brothers Grocery and Hardware store at Second and Main Streets. They took over the store on June 15, 1891. In 1916, they moved to 316 Main Street, and for many years, the store was the oldest business in Galena operating continuously under the same management. The brothers sold the store in April 1954.

J.T. Goodman's bakery opened at Third and Main Streets in 1905 and soon moved to 704 Main Street. Goodman once had an employee arrested because, "while in an intoxicated state," the man burned $50 worth of bread. Goodman's wife, Ruth, took over after he died, and her business became the hardware and feed store in 1938. Ruth ended up spending six decades in business on the same block and died at age 97 in 1976.

Ulrich "Ferd" Ferdinand ran a tailor shop in Galena for over 30 years. He took over the shop at 309 Main Street after owner J.A. Moore, who had incurred a large pile of debt, simply packed his things and disappeared one day in 1913. Ferdinand advertised that he carried "a complete line of imported and domestic woolens" and that "if your prices are too high come to Galena."

This 1899 Ancient Order of United Workmen (AOUW) parade passes Moses Baum's Dry Goods at Third and Main Streets. Baum's opened in 1877, just a few weeks after lead was discovered. The store was later located at Sixth and Main Streets and was operated by son Leo Baum. The AOUW was a fraternal order organized in part to provide life insurance to workers and had 6,000 lodges at the time.

In this view looking south on Main Street from Fourth Street during the 1950s, the Golden Rule Store is visible at left. Generations of area families shopped at the store founded by J.S. Barnes in 1877. Ted Senter took over in 1915, and his daughter Dorotha ran the store from 1973 until closing in 1998. The Citizen's Bank of Galena occupied the building on the right. The building later became a bar named the Golden Hawk.

Main Street and Galena as a whole is undergoing a revival today, due in part to Route 66 tourism and the determination of the locals. New businesses are opening, and the improved streetscape includes nostalgic lampposts and street signs. This photograph with a view looking south from Fourth Street was taken in August 2012. At that time, Galena was hosting a celebration in conjunction with the International Route 66 Festival in Joplin.

Dr. Clem H. Jones spent over 50 years serving the area and is said to have delivered 5,000 babies. He practiced at Baxter Springs for eight years before coming to Galena in 1900. During one of Jones's three terms as mayor of Galena, his brother Dr. Charles Jones also served as the mayor of Baxter Springs. A third brother was a mayor in Longton, Kansas.

Dr. Clem H. Jones's first office was above the old First National Bank Building at Fourth and Main Streets, and he later moved to Fourth and Short Streets. He drove a horse and buggy until 1913. Dr. Jones is shown here with the new horseless carriage at his home at 314 Short Street. He died at home in 1950. The house still stands.

Up to 175 women were employed by the Galena Shirt Company, one of several satellite factories of the D.M. Oberman Manufacturing Company of Joplin. The firm originally intended to buy the landmark Century Hotel for the factory, but the deal fell through. Instead, it was established in the former Best Place Dry Goods Company at 515–516 Main Street in 1920.

In 1905, the V. West Meat Market at 607 West Main Street was sold to John Volz, who owned his own farm and slaughterhouse west of Galena. The photograph was retouched in later years to reflect the name change. J.H. Cooper later ran the business, and John Volz later ran the North End Meat Market at 105 Main Street.

Robert "Bob" Brown's Standard Oil service station sits on an angle on the northwest corner of Fifth and Main Streets. The station, with its big canopy and support columns, closed in the mid-1970s and sat vacant for over 10 years; however, the expanded and remodeled building became a Mexican restaurant.

Howard "Pappy" Litch was born in 1906 near Hell's Half Acre and was just 11 years old when his mother died. His father would not marry again for fear another woman would not be as devoted to his child. Howard quit school to help support his dad, who would not permit him to work in the mines. Litch (left) is shown here working at Kennedy Auto when it was on Main Street.

Pappy Litch opened his own garage in 1937 and had built a successful business when his draft notice came in 1943. Howard married Ruby Shears before he left. When he returned after the war, Litch's old garage had been rented, and he started over at this location on West Seventh Street. This building was later a TV repair shop and eventually became the Cornerstone Alternative Charter High School.

In 1954, Pappy Litch took over a former livery stable at Fifth and Main Streets that had also once housed the Fifth Street Garage. Howard retired in 1974 and the garage was sold, but the new owner kept the original sign intact. The old building was severely damaged by a storm and demolished in February 1996. The corner is now part of Howard "Pappy" Litch Park.

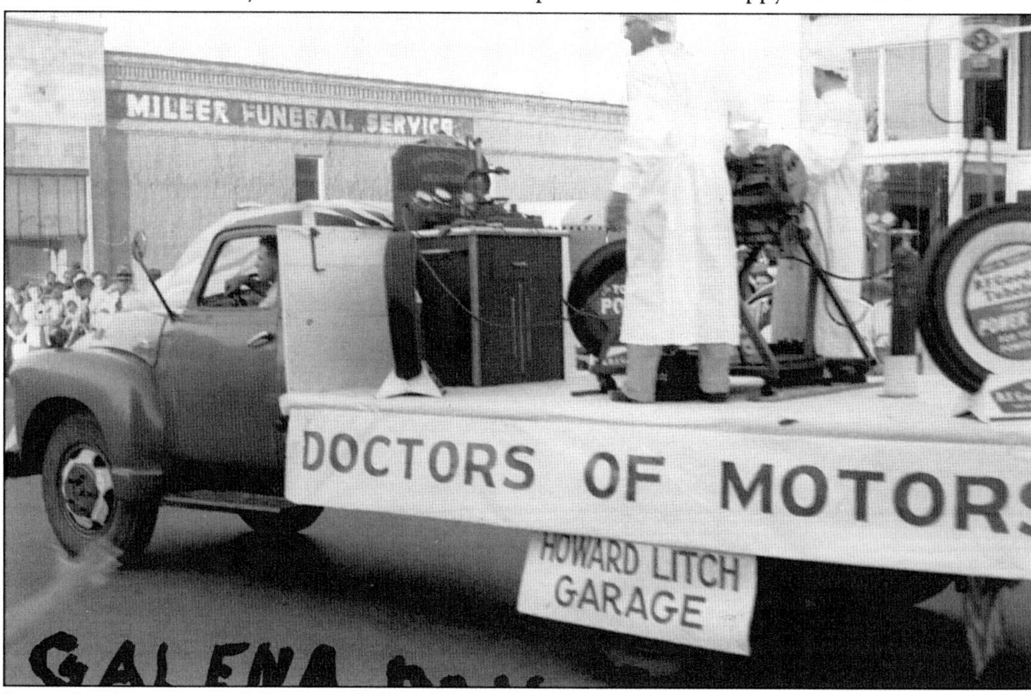

Pappy Litch was one of the most beloved figures in town. He spent a lifetime collecting artifacts from Galena's history and preserving the heritage of the Tri-State Mining District. Litch stored the treasures in sheds, hoping some day to house it all in a museum. This photograph from his collection shows some of the employees of the Litch Garage taking part in the 1955 Galena Days as "Doctors of Motors."

In 1983, Pappy Litch got his wish when Bill Hall purchased the MKT Depot and donated it for a municipal museum. The depot was moved next to the municipal complex, and the Galena Mining and Historical Museum opened in 1984 with Litch as founder and curator. He died on November 6, 1996, and dedicated volunteers staff the museum today.

The local chamber of commerce and other community members donated the land for Howard "Pappy" Litch Memorial Park in 2001. A Will Rogers Highway marker, dedicated at the state line in 1952, was moved to the park and is now located at the base of this second-generation monument detailing some of the history. The small park includes green space, flagpoles, and a gazebo.

The Galena Volunteer Fire Department was organized in August 1889. The newspaper was proud of the "lusty volunteers." To summon them, a 1,200-pound bell was put up on a 60-foot-high tower at city hall, at that time located at Fifth and Main Streets. These volunteers pose with the department's first fire truck, purchased in 1912 at a cost of $5,000.

The members of the Galena volunteer fire department pose with their equipment around 1950. Pappy Litch is the first firefighter to the left of the man in street clothes at center. The building in the background is Liberty School, completed in 1941. It now houses Liberty Elementary and the Galena Middle School.

For 48 years, Pappy Litch also served as a Galena volunteer firefighter, including stints as chief and assistant chief. On August 9, 1951, Litch helped rescue the injured 17-year-old Gene McCumber after the child fell into an old mine shaft known as "Pigeon Cave" on West Fifth Street. He helped the boy into a bucket lowered by the Litch Garage tow truck.

The Galena police officers in this 1947 photograph are not identified, but records show Fred Bever was the Galena police chief at the time. Robert Todd and Ray Means were among the patrolmen, and Augie Gilstrap was the assistant chief. Means nearly lost his life when a fleeing suspect fell down a mine shaft to his death. The officer fell 50 feet trying to save the man.

The city constructed a new building in 1902 on Main Street to house administrative offices, the fire and police departments, the courtroom, the jail, and the library. It received a new facade in the early 1970s. Galena City Hall was moved to West Seventh Street in the 1970s, and the cupola that housed the fire bell sits rotting away in a lot just west of the Eagle-Picher smelter.

Lawyer, judge, and politician Edward E. Sapp was one of Galena's leading citizens and erected the Sapp Opera House in 1890. The 900-seat theater stood on the southeast corner of Seventh and Main Streets and hosted plays, concerts, boxing matches, and an appearance by Harry Houdini. He made his debut as a "spiritualist" there on January 8, 1898. The opera house was destroyed by a fire on March 8, 1931.

Brothers Frank H., Shelton H., and Cassius L. Rohrbough operated their oil and gas business and ran one of the first filling stations in town. Rohrbough Brothers opened at 710 Main Street in 1918, and their truck is shown here backed up to the curbside pump during the 1920s. In a view looking north from Eighth and Main Streets, the Sapp Opera House is in the background at right.

An extremely rare Kansas Route 66 shield shows the way in this 1931 view of Seventh Street looking east at Main Street. On the right side of the street at the corner, the ruins of the Sapp Opera House can be seen. Another sign points the way to the City Café. At left, a makeshift Route 66 sign is posted on a telephone pole in front of the McCartney-Kennedy Drug Store.

A slightly earlier view looking east on Seventh Street at Main Street shows an unusual stop sign simply stuck in the pavement. A row of birds crosses the route. To the left on Seventh Street are the curbside gas pumps in front of the Chevrolet dealership that later became the Kennedy Auto Company. Note the trolley tracks.

Val Richards constructed this ornate building on the northwest corner of Sixth and Main Streets in 1893 and served as mayor in 1893–1894. His old house is now the Derfelt Funeral Home. At the time this photograph was taken, the Richards Building was the McCartney-Kennedy Drug Store, but it is best remembered as the location of Schwartz Drug, operated by Otto and Laurena Schwartz.

Glen Harreld, owner of the Harreld Photography Studio, captured busy downtown Galena in this view, which is looking north from the 700 block of South Main Street. The Richards Building on the right had not yet received its modern facade, and the Willis Market still occupied the southeast corner of the Seventh and South Main Streets intersection. The market is now gone, and that corner is vacant.

The corner of Seventh and Main Streets had a very different look by the 1950s, when the Main Street facade of the Richards Building and the Ida Block was modernized and faced with brick. In 1963, Route 66 was moved off Main Street but still passed through this intersection, as the new alignment followed Seventh Street.

Margaret E. Largent Montee, Miss Galena of 1952, rides up Main Street in a brand-new Oldsmobile past the Willis Market. Almon Willis operated the market on the former site of the Sapp Opera House from 1939 until 1960. He served as mayor in 1954–1955. The Galena Assembly of God Church and the Galena Journal Building are also visible. The market site is now a vacant lot. (Courtesy of Dale Largent.)

The Galena Assembly of God started out in 1903, holding services in the Grand Leader Building on Main Street and the Pearl Theater at 710 Main Street. In 1915, the church moved to 711 Main Street. In the 1950s, the congregation met in front to celebrate after the original structure was expanded and covered with brick. Note the neon cross.

By the time this 1957 photograph with a view looking north on Main Street towards Seventh Street was taken, the Assembly of God church had expanded again and had added a new facade. The church relocated to East Seventh Street in 1980 and later moved to Fifth Street. The building shown here became the Saints Memorial Church of God in Christ.

Thomas Kennedy Sr. owned the local Ford agency on Main Street until he died in June 1923 and his sons Richard and Claude assumed operation of the dealership. In July 1930, the Kennedy Auto Company moved to the former Hulse Garage at 115 East Seventh Street, shown here. The back of the Richards Building is at left, and the Seventh Street Buffet and Bar is on the right.

The City Café was located on the west side of Main Street, one-half block south of Seventh Street. The men behind the counter in this 1922 photograph are identified as Ivan Carney (left), Dwight Irby (center), and 16-year-old Bob Brown.

The Galena Meat Market was located on the west side of Main Street in the Liberty Hall, which also served as the Independent Order of Odd Fellows Lodge. The men behind the counter in the picture, which dates from about 1925, are Roy Tremble (left), Fred Archer (center), and Harry Gray. Liberty Hall was completely renovated in 2015 and now features a floor covered with pennies.

In 2012, the two buildings on the southwest corner of Seventh and Main Streets were demolished to improve the intersection. A concrete wall was constructed for a mural made of tiles, funded by local businessman Brian Jordan and designed by Chris Auckerman and John White of Images in Tile. A park was added to allow Route 66 travelers to take time for a photo opportunity.

Civic leader Clarence G. Worthington operated the Star Grocery, established in 1898. He later formed a successful insurance agency and was involved in real estate. Worthington also served as secretary of the Galena Commercial Club. The men in the photograph are unidentified.

In the summer of 1880, a group met in a brush arbor on the banks of Short Creek and agreed to organize the First Christian Church of Galena. The first permanent building was on Joplin Street between Fourth and Fifth Streets. That structure was moved to Tenth and Main Streets in 1898 and forms the auditorium today. The bell tower was added shortly after the move.

The First Baptist Church, founded the same year that the City of Galena was incorporated, was originally known as the First Baptist Church of Short Creek. The building with the neon biblical sign, which has since been replaced, was constructed on the former site of the East Galena School at Seventh Street and Euclid Avenue after World War II.

The Methodist Episcopal church at Fifth and Joplin Streets was constructed in 1908. It is shown here in 1918, during the funeral for Bernard Parks, the first soldier from Galena to die during World War I. Parks died when the three-inch gun he was loading exploded during a training exercise at Fort Sill, Oklahoma. In 1969, the church one block off Route 66 became the United Methodist Church of Galena.

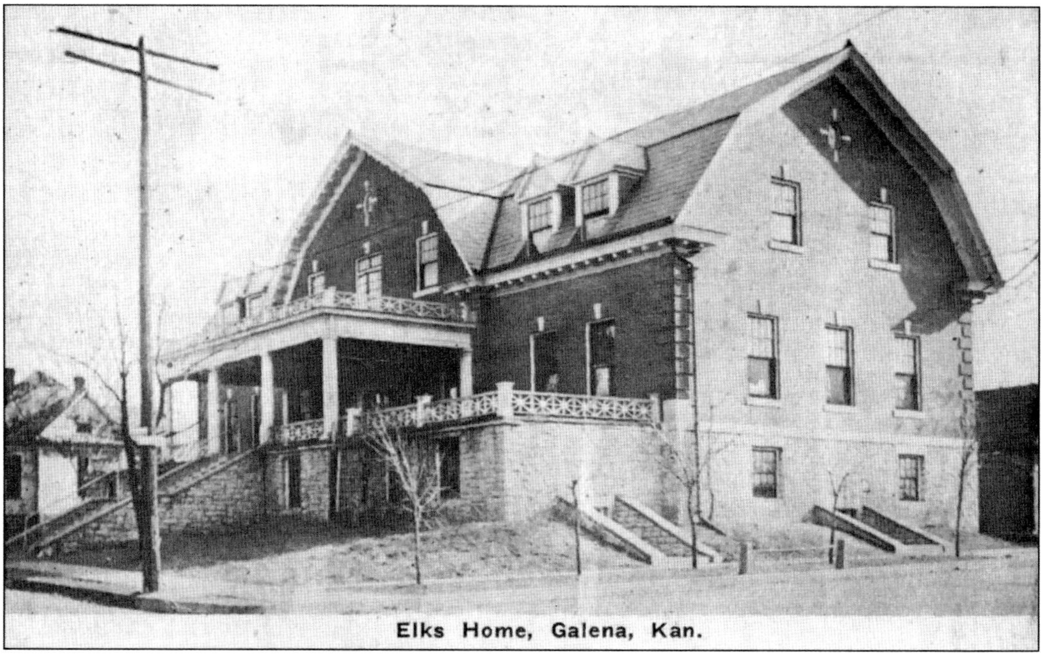

The Benevolent and Protective Order of Elks Lodge No. 677 at Galena was founded in July 1906. The fraternal organization's lodge at Seventh and Joplin Streets was constructed next to the Sapp Opera House that same year at a cost of $15,000. It was described as one of the finest in the state and is still used by the organization today.

During a century of mining in the Tri-State District of Missouri, Kansas, and Oklahoma, more than 4,000 mines produced 23 million tons of zinc and 4 million tons of lead ore. That was 50 percent of the zinc and 10 percent of the lead produced in the United States. The last mine in the district, located west of Baxter Springs, closed in 1970. These men worked in the Jackrabbit Mine at Galena.

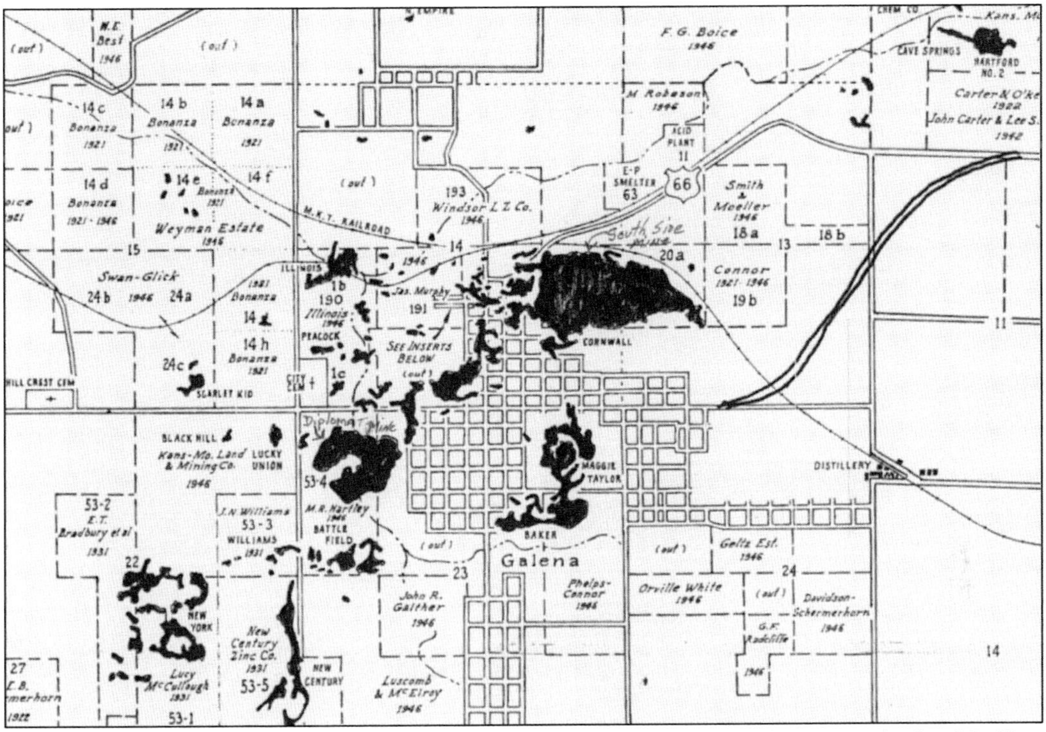

This map shows the locations of some of the 800 mine shafts around Galena. Hundreds of shallow lead and zinc mines under the city are collapsing and threatening buildings on Main Street. In 2006, a collapse damaged the 114-year-old structure housing the Green Parrot Bar, the last bar in downtown Galena. The building had to be demolished.

The Galena Lead and Zinc Company's Diplomat Mine covered a large area bounded roughly by Seventh Street, Dewey Street, Eleventh Street, and Schermerhorn Road. It was one of the most productive mines within the Galena city limits and closed in 1922. Besides the softball fields, much of the land over the Diplomat Mine has remained undeveloped, due to the risk of cave-ins.

These Galena miners pose with a box of dynamite and an air-powered piston drill. The drill was usually mounted on a pedestal and drilled holes usually about eight feet deep for placement of the dynamite. Once the blast was over, the shovelers moved in to place the dirt and ore into buckets that could hold up to 1,500 pounds for transportation to the surface.

Miner's wages were low and the work was hard and often deadly. In addition to the collapses, explosions, and other accidents, there was a good chance a miner would develop silicosis from breathing in the dust. The Tri-State Mining District had the highest rates of tuberculosis in the country. Miners and their families became ill from crowded conditions and substandard housing, such as this strip miner's shack in Cherokee County. (Courtesy of Library of Congress.)

Mining left the ground contaminated with heavy metals like lead, zinc, and cadmium and the flooded mine shafts leaked acidic water into streams. Children were injured or killed playing around the open shafts and the piles of chat, such as those shown here in 1980. Since the mining companies have all folded, local, state, and federal agencies have faced the task of cleaning up. The EPA has removed the contaminated soil from 650 properties in Galena.

An interurban electric streetcar system linked Galena and Baxter Springs with Carthage and Joplin in Missouri and Picher, Oklahoma. It all started with a mule car line between Webb City and Carterville, Missouri, in 1889 that developed into the Southwest Missouri Electric Railway. The line and its branches would stretch from Carthage, Missouri, to Picher, Oklahoma, and cars ran every half hour.

In 1918, Southwest Missouri Railroad officials got into a dispute with Galena leaders over the route and bypassed the town a couple of blocks to the south before connecting with Baxter Springs and Picher. A branch line, including this "Dinkey" car, did serve Galena along the state line, Mineral Avenue, Seventh Street, and Main Street. The interurban line shut down in 1939.

Many early motorists shunned the fancy hotels in the cities and often just pulled off to the side of the road to camp. Farmers soon had their fill of the "tin can tourists" and some cities constructed tourist parks. Galena's municipal tourist park was opened in 1922 and located on a three-acre site in what is now Schermerhorn Park. Motorists could pull off the road, take a dip in Shoal Creek, and camp for the night.

Jack Martin's Sovereign Service station was on West Seventh Street at Elm Street. From left to right are Jack and his sons Gerald and Hap. The station offered Kansas and Missouri stickers in the days when crossing a state line was worthy of a souvenir. The building was faced with giraffe rock, flat rocks with grout in the seams, a style very common in the Ozarks. A glass company stands on the site today.

The Galena Roller Rink was a half mile west of town on Highway 66. Leo Williams ran the grocery store at Riverton for 25 years before he retired and took over the rink in 1943. His wife, Lora, ran the rink after he died in 1948. It was also later owned by Fred Zeigler and Lee and Anna May Adams. The rink hosted hockey games, square dances, and a 1951 New Year's Eve Party for "Colored Folk" on January 2. Fire destroyed the rink in July 1961. (Steve Rider.)

The Camp Joy Tourist Camp opened about 1927 atop a rise that would become known as Camp Joy Hill, located two miles west of Galena. Fire destroyed some of the complex, which is shown here in November 1940. Owners of Camp Joy included R.E. Guinn, Dan Isley, and Claude C. Card. It became the Camp Joy Trading Post in the 1960s and was a flea market into the 1970s.

The first schoolhouse in the area was a log cabin on Short Creek in Hickory Flats that was constructed in 1873. The building at upper left is the old high school at Fifth and Chicago Streets, which opened in 1904 and was demolished in 1973. Clockwise from upper right are the Spring Grove School, Columbia School, and Central School.

At the height of the Great Depression, a government program for unemployed teachers set up an emergency nursery school at the vacant Columbia School. Beginning in 1934, the program cared for two- to five-year-olds and fed them during the day. There were 12 such schools in the state, and Galena had the largest, with up to 100 students at a time. Columbia School was located at Fourth and Short Streets but no longer stands.

Edgar Backers Schermerhorn arrived in Galena with 50¢ in his pocket in 1877. He was the richest man in Cherokee County when he died in 1923. The civic leader and philanthropist invested in real estate and served as president of the Citizen's State Bank. In 1875, he built a home named the Galena Belle at 805 East Fifth Street that still stands today.

On June 21, 1922, Edgar Schermerhorn deeded 22 scenic acres on Shoal Creek south of Galena to the city for use as a park. During the Depression, the Works Progress Administration (WPA) built a stone structure known as the Scout Cabin in addition to attractive terraces and walls. This footbridge spanned Shoal Creek at the park but was lost in the flood of 1943. From left to right are Harry Wright, Ben Moody, and city engineer W.L. Ricksecker.

The old Scout Cabin atop the hill in Schermerhorn Park now houses the Southeast Kansas Nature Center and is filled with exhibits on the animals and plants of the region known as the Kansas Ozarks as well as a large collection of Native American artifacts. There are plenty of hands-on activities for children, and Schermerhorn Cave is home to several species of endangered salamanders. A small portion of the cave entrance can be viewed.

Fred "Boodle" Lane started out as a miner but preferred the dangerous practice of "scrapping." Scrappers entered old mines alone, removed leftover galena, and scoured the mine tailing dumps for sphalerite. In 1927, he added a few minerals to the tables outside his roadside grocery store and drink stand. He was delighted when tourists snapped up the glittering crystallized calcite and dolomite, considered waste rock by the miners.

BOODLE'S MINERAL SPECIMENS. ONE MILE WEST OF GALENA, KANSAS

The modestly priced items were displayed in the yard, but Boodle Lane kept the rarities in a shed. His second wife, Lois Faye, helped out with the business. However, Boodle was much more than a roadside merchant. He shipped specimens around the world and is credited with saving tons of priceless minerals from being crushed. He died in 1962, but his specimens grace countless museums and prominent collections today.

Three

Riverton

There were three Marsh arch bridges on Route 66 in Kansas, named for the designer, James Barney Marsh. Pictured is the 525-foot-long structure with three spans across the Spring River; it was built in 1921 and demolished in 1986. A smaller Marsh arch bridge carrying Route 66 over Willow Creek met a similar fate in 1991. The Brush Creek Bridge to the west is the only Marsh arch bridge remaining on Route 66 in Kansas. (Courtesy of Kansas Department of Transportation.)

James McDowell constructed a home on the west side of the Spring River in 1902. In 1905, he sold it for $1,500 to the newly established Joplin Country Club. A spur from the electric streetcar railway served the club, which offered boating, a swimming pool, tennis courts, and picnic areas. Use of the club declined during the Depression, and the home was sold to club president J.W. Grantham and his wife, Pearl, in 1932.

The Granthams sold the 88-acre Joplin Country Club site and the home to the Harreld family in 1953, and June Harreld turned the home into the Spring River Inn, which opened in 1954. The inn had six private dining areas, one of which could seat over 350 guests, and was famous for its huge buffet, fried chicken, cinnamon bubble pull-apart bread, and squaw bread.

Judy and Ray Birk ran the Spring River Inn from 1970 until 1994, when it was sold to a partnership of David and Kay Graham and Dewayne and Lavern Treece. The Spring River Inn closed down in 1996, and the landmark was destroyed by fire on October 20, 1998. The sign that stood at the entrance had been removed and was undergoing restoration in 2016.

At the turn of the 20th century, electrical power was replacing some of the hard labor in the mining district. To meet the demand, the Spring River Power Company (predecessor of the Empire District Electric Company) built Lowell Dam on the Spring River at its confluence with Shoal Creek in 1904. The dam created Lake Lowell. The hydroelectric plant went on line on March 4, 1905, but it is no longer in operation. (Empire District Electric Company.)

Some warned that a dam at Lowell would not last. Following a washout in 1909, the Spring River was routed through a bypass a mile to the north, and a bridge with 83 floodgates was built there. Some called it the "I Told You So" bridge. The main structure no longer stands, but the spillway forms Empire Dam Falls, the largest man-made waterfall in Kansas. The falls are about one mile south of Route 66 on Southeast Seventieth Street.

In 1909, the Empire District Electric Company began construction of the Riverton Generating Station. The plant originally used a 400-ton, 5,000-horsepower generator dubbed "Old Kate" that had produced electricity at the 1904 World's Fair in St. Louis. Today's massive plant uses natural gas instead of coal and can generate 286 megawatts.

Riverton is an unincorporated community that was originally a Quaker settlement. When a post office was applied for, residents wanted to name it Varrick, but the post office shortened it to "Varck." The name was changed after the Empire District Electric plant was constructed. The former Riverton Grocery building still stands.

Record flooding was underway along the Spring River in May 1943 as this guard kept watch at the Jayhawk Ordnance Plant northwest of Galena. The Boston Mills Bridge is in the background. Part of Route 66 was washed out, 5,000 miners were out of work, and the Empire District Electric plant at Riverton was flooded. The ordnance plant produced ammonium nitrate and is now the Jayhawk Fine Chemicals Corporation facility.

Leo and Lora Williams opened a general store at Riverton on March 20, 1925, that they dubbed the Y-Not-Eat Bar-B-Q. It included a croquet court, later converted to a parking lot, and a Standard service station. Leo was a charter member of the 66 Highway Association and renamed the store the Leo Williams Grocery in the 1940s.

Leo Williams took over the Galena Roller Rink in 1943 and leased the store to Lloyd Paxton. After Leo died and the lease expired in 1948, Lora Williams returned and operated the store as an AG Market. Joe and Isabelle Eisler bought the store in 1973. Their nephew Scott Nelson runs the Eisler Brothers Market today, and it looks much the same with its tin ceiling, shelves lined with antiques and sundries, and the old soda-pop cooler.

Old Route 66 continues straight west at Routes 400 and 89A as Beasley Road. This short segment leads to the Marsh arch bridge on Brush Creek, known as the Rainbow Bridge. In 1992, this bridge was endangered as a bypass was being constructed for local traffic; however, the Kansas Historic Route 66 Association mobilized to save the historic bridge.

This group visited the Brush Creek Rainbow Bridge while it was under construction in 1923. From left to right are construction superintendent Charles Mosier, Charles Mosier Jr., Duane Thompson, Anna (Shaffer) Mosier, Wayne Shaffer, Mae Thompson, Jay Crane, Gladys (Mosier) Wilson (sitting), and Ruby Thompson (the little girl).

For many years, Brush Creek Bridge was known as "Graffiti Bridge," and scrawling names on the span was a local tradition. The Kansas Historic Route 66 Association and the Cherokee County Commission joined together to make repairs in 1994. A National Park Service Route 66 Corridor Preservation grant helped with additional work on the superstructure in 2005.

The concrete road from Galena to Riverton opened on August 4, 1922. These crews worked for the Koss Construction Company of Des Moines, Iowa, which started paving the 4.6 miles between Riverton and Baxter Springs in 1923. Another firm completed the Marsh arch bridges at Willow Creek and Brush Creek in January 1924, and the entire road was ready in the spring.

Four

THE MILITARY ROAD

In what is now southeastern Kansas, a spring once flowed from a hill near the Military Road, linking Fort Leavenworth in Kansas and Fort Gibson in the Indian Territory. The area was still closed to white settlers when John Baxter arrived with his wife and eight children in 1849. He ran an inn and store called Baxter's Place. Another illegal settler killed Baxter in a land dispute in 1859, but Baxter's name lived on in the community, shown here in an early drawing. (Library of Congress.)

During the Civil War, a small fort was established at the springs and named for Col. Charles W. Blair, federal commander of the District of Southern Kansas and Fort Scott. The fort was also referred to as "Fort Baxter" and "Baxter Springs." It was manned by about 150 men, approximately 75 of whom were with the 2nd Kansas Colored Infantry. This reconstruction of the fort is located north of the Baxter Springs Heritage Center.

Notorious guerilla William Clarke Quantrill and his men attacked Fort Blair on October 6, 1863, and were beaten back by the outnumbered defenders. But outside the fort, the guerillas came upon a detachment of mostly African American troops escorting Maj. Gen. James G. Blunt. The rebels killed at least 82 soldiers, many in cold blood, as they tried to surrender. This mural of the battle by Ed Ness is located at the Baxter Springs Heritage Center.

Quantrill's raiders were disguised as federal troops, so General Blunt's band was preparing a musical welcome when the attack came. The musicians were massacred as they pleaded for their lives, and their bodies were burned. Blunt somehow escaped and is shown at right in this photograph taken in 1864 with his replacement band. He was later removed from command and died in an insane asylum in 1881.

In 1869, the federal government wanted to move the victims of the Baxter Springs Massacre from the battlefield to a national cemetery in Springfield, Missouri. Instead, the community donated what is now known as the National Block in the middle of the city cemetery, two miles west of town, and agreed to maintain it forever. The men killed in the massacre were reinterred there. The monument was dedicated on Decoration Day in 1886. (Courtesy of Library of Congress.)

In this 1931 photograph, Capt. F.A.W. Arnold (right) poses with Mayor Sam Douthit at the new Quantrill's Raid monument placed by local Daughters of the American Revolution. It still stands on the grounds of the Johnston Library. Captain Arnold survived despite being shot in the face and left for dead. He went on to become the postmaster and a newspaper editor in Lamar, Missouri.

On July 21, 1878, Chief Joseph and 410 weary and sick members of the persecuted Nez Perce tribe arrived by rail at Baxter Springs for relocation to the nearby Quapaw Agency in the Indian Territory (present-day Oklahoma), where many died of epidemic diseases. Although those still living were returned to the Pacific Northwest in 1885, Chief Joseph and half of his band were never allowed to return to their homeland in Idaho.

From 1883 until 1914, up to 80,000 people annually attended the weeklong Old Soldiers and Sailors Reunions of the Grand Army of the Republic, a Union Civil War veterans organization. The reunions took place on a 100-acre site on the Spring River in southeast Baxter Springs known as Camp Logan. Each morning, the roar of the cannon would start the day.

During the reunions, thousands of families set up camp on the hillsides surrounding the grounds. The reunion association provided free tents, straw, and 80 acres for parking teams of horses. Camp Logan was served by a two-mile spur of the Frisco Railroad and had its own daily newspaper. Steve and Ella Etter of the Etter Bakery in Baxter Springs were among the vendors, advertising "our bread can be buttered but not bettered."

Red Hot Street at Camp Logan offered a half mile of sideshows, eating establishments, vendors, games, and amusements and included branch offices of newspapers from around the nation. Today, modern homes built along Oak Crest Circle and Oak Lane stand on the site of the former reunion grounds, and no trace of the once lively Red Hot Street remains.

The *John Logan* was an electric-powered boat that offered excursions on the Spring River during the Grand Army of the Republic reunions. Gen. John Alexander Logan was the third commander in chief of the Grand Army of the Republic (GAR) who issued the 1868 order declaring May 30 as Decoration Day, which is now known as Memorial Day.

The Shoot the Chutes was an amusement ride at Camp Logan that took advantage of the steep hillside; the top was at the east end of present-day Oak Lane. The midway, or "Pike," also included a grand carousel, electric fountain, scenic railway, high dive, Loop-the-Loop, Slide for Life, and other attractions billed by the GAR as "thrilling and astounding devices of the 20th Century."

These veterans were ready to keep order among the former soldiers, sailors, cowboys, preachers, and pioneer families attending the reunions. These members of the Old Soldiers' Reunion Police Force are, from left to right, George Cravens, Tom King, unidentified, Matt Clary, Walt Sullivan, H.S. Roberson, C.B. Puterbaugh, George Stoskopf, and unidentified.

Local lore says life was cheap, and many a badman swung from the "Hanging Tree" during the cowtown days in Baxter Springs. It was located between Sixth and Seventh Streets, about a half block east of Military Avenue. The reconstruction of Fort Blair now stands here. At the time of this 1954 photograph, the old elm was succumbing to disease and drought.

Five

Baxter Springs

Baxter Springs was the "First Cowtown in Kansas," a destination for cattle drives at the end of the Eastern Shawnee Trail. The boom only lasted a couple of years before fear of disease pushed the cattle drives farther west to towns such as Dodge City and Abilene. This welcome sign was erected on Route 66 by the chamber of commerce and the local Kiwanis Club.

The longhorn steer, once so important to Baxter Springs, had largely disappeared by 1938 when Col. Wilbur Avery unveiled a life-size statue of the animal. Avery was a cowboy who struck it rich in mining and established two western museums at his West Twin Ranch southwest of Baxter Springs. The land and his collections were auctioned off for over $3 million in 2007.

German immigrant Edward Zellekin established his brewery at the springs in 1870 to serve the thirsty cowtown. He abandoned it after the cattle boom ended and moved to Joplin, Missouri, to make his fortune in mining. In 1892, Charles E. Parham turned the old brewery into the headquarters of his Apostolic Faith Movement. It was torn down in the early 1960s.

After the cattle trade moved on, the population of Baxter Springs plummeted to about 800, but the supposed curative powers of the springs made the town a tourist destination. The lavish Wiggins House was built on the northwest corner of Ninth Street and Military Avenue during the "spa era." It was also known as the Planters and became the Springs Hotel. The hotel and saloon burned down in 1912. The springs dried up in the 1920s, probably due to mining activity.

During the Baxter Springs spa era, pagodas were built over the springs and a springs bathhouse was constructed on the southeast corner of Seventh Street and Military Avenue. E.E. Long took this photograph as the 1895 flood began to recede. Years later, a home was built on the site of the bathhouse, but it was wiped out by the flood of 1993.

In 1868, an election rife with fraud on both sides made Columbus the Cherokee County Seat. The citizens of Baxter Springs authorized construction of the courthouse and jail (above) in a futile attempt to win it back. It was completed in 1872 and is shown here on Decoration Day in 1883. Prisoners were held in the basement until the county jail was completed at Columbus in 1880.

The courthouse building would serve as city hall, a church, a college, and a theater where the first movies in town were shown in 1898. Civic leader and Swedish immigrant Peter Nils Johnston left $5,000 for establishment of a public library, and the city donated the building in 1905. The Johnston Library opened on October 1, 1907, and still serves patrons today.

The Civil War cannon that stood in front of the old city hall and Johnston Library can be seen today at the Baxter Springs Heritage Center. Dave Hurt is shown here in June 1950 after he rebuilt the wheels on the Confederate Napoleon cannon. Hurt worked as a blacksmith in Baxter Springs for over 50 years.

A twister on July 5, 1895, killed five people, tossed railroad cars off the tracks, and destroyed a church. John Cooper's Dry Goods Store, located on the northwest corner of Twelfth Street and Military Avenue, would be repaired. The building later housed the Ritz Theater, the Blue Castle Restaurant, and Baxter Floral. A tornado also did extensive damage in Baxter Springs in 2014.

Military Avenue was bustling when this view was captured in 1917 at the height of the mining boom. Several of the vehicles in this photograph belonged to the Atlas Powder Company, a major supplier to the mining industry. Baxter Springs reaped many of the economic benefits of the mines, but suffered less environmental damage than some other communities, because the Baxter Springs City Council banned mining within the city limits. Many mining executives, however, made their homes in town.

The Ballard Mine was the largest of the mines in the immediate Baxter Springs area, located on West Nineteenth Street. Others included the Hartley, Brewster, and Swalley Mines. The Estes family, African American pioneers, owned a mine southwest of town that employed 25 black men. Very few African Americans were given opportunities in the other mines.

The Eagle-Picher Central Mill was constructed on Route 66 between Baxter Springs and Commerce, Oklahoma, about 1932. The tailing, or chat, pile was over 400 feet high and was said to be the largest in the country. Chat piles like this still exist in nearby Treece, Kansas, and Picher, Oklahoma. Many claim these piles are to blame for health issues in these towns.

Much of the ore from the Tri-State (Missouri, Kansas, and Oklahoma) Mining District was shipped to the Eagle-Picher Central Mill to be processed. In the 1970s, processing ceased at the mill, and the mining boom in the area was over. Eventually, the huge tailing piles here were hauled away, and many of the buildings were torn down.

The massive chat piles and mines deep under the earth were something of a tourist attraction in the Tri-State Mining District. The Oklahoma Mine, a couple of miles south of Baxter Springs on Highway 66, offered tours of the abandoned shaft at $1.25 for adults and 65¢ for children. Advertisements noted the temperature was a constant 54 degrees inside the old mine.

Mine tours offered views of the many lakes, underground railways, and roads big enough for tractor trailers beneath the Tri-State Mining District. These tourists are inside the Nancy Jane Mine, located off Route 66 and southwest of Baxter Springs near Commerce, Oklahoma. Claude Donica started the tours in 1950 and named the mine after his daughter.

In addition to the lead and zinc, southeast Kansas also produced vast amounts of coal, usually removed by strip mining. A 15-story-high Bucyrus-Erie model 1850B electric shovel dubbed "Big Brutus" could remove three railcar loads of coal in one swoop. It was in operation from 1962 until 1973. Too big to move or dismantle, Big Brutus seemed doomed to rust away until it was restored and turned into a museum near West Mineral.

Mickey Charles Mantle was born in Spavinaw, Oklahoma, on October 20, 1931. A few years later, his family moved to Commerce, Oklahoma, a few miles south of Baxter Springs on Route 66. Mickey's father was a lead miner who loved baseball and taught his son well. Working for Eagle-Picher during the summer months, Mickey became amazingly strong. By age 16, he was playing with the semipro Whiz Kids team from Baxter Springs.

Mickey Mantle, third from right, and the Whiz Kids played at Kiwanis Park on Route 166, just west of the Spring River. In 1948, a New York Yankees' scout came to see one of Mickey's teammates, but Mickey stole the show by slugging two pitches into the river, one from each side of the plate. The impressed scout returned in 1949 when Mickey graduated from high school and signed him to a minor-league contract. The old stadium no longer stands.

Mickey's business venture at the end of the Oklahoma Turnpike was a big hit. He was a co-owner of the Mickey Mantle Holiday Inn on south Rangeline in Joplin from 1957 until 1965. Some of his memorabilia was on display at the hotel's Dugout Room, the first "sports bar" in the Tri-State area.

Baxter Springs is still crazy for youth baseball. The Little League teams have won numerous state titles, and the current Little League stadium (shown here) is one of the finest in the nation. A Little League museum next to the field showcases Mickey Mantle items as well as memorabilia from golfer Hale Irwin, who also played Little League ball here.

North of Baxter Springs on Route 66, Karnes Stadium at the Field of Dreams hosts high school and American Legion games. Coach Don Karnes organized the local high school team in 1981 and the American Legion program in 1982. In 1999, Karnes and his wife, Betty, donated the land and formed a nonprofit organization to get the stadium constructed. It was dedicated on April 30, 2015.

In 1927, Raymond Cook and Walter Swalley formed a group of Boy Scouts into a troop of synchronized riders named for movie star cowboy Tom Mix. Their performances were so popular that Mix came to town and is at center in this photograph, wearing a white hat. The Tom Mix Patrol evolved into the Mounted Troops of America, which had clubs all over the Southwest.

Baxter Springs constable and chief of police W. T. Bridges and his men are shown here after a 1929 raid on a still. Being a lawman in Baxter Springs was a dangerous occupation. The first town marshal, M.C. Seaman, was killed during a disturbance involving a "woman of ill repute" at the Wiggins House in 1870. The second marshal, C.M. Taylor, was killed while attempting to arrest the mayor over a debt in 1872.

The original Lincoln School was built in 1872, a block northeast of the building that became the Johnston Library. The impressive school building cost $25,000 and was known for its large bell, now displayed at the Baxter Springs Heritage Center. This photograph was taken in 1957 after the new Lincoln School had opened but before the old one was demolished.

The population of Baxter Springs peaked at about 10,000 during the cowtown days and then began to fall rapidly. But the population exploded during the mining era. By 1917, the population was four times larger than it had been in 1915. Six miles of city streets were paved in 1918. Three years later, there was another boom when the Picher mining field opened up.

Baxter Springs merchants offered special deals and prizes during a Booster Day on April 1, 1911. The J.P. Opperman Harness and Saddle Shop is visible on the left, one of the last remnants of the cowtown era. Opperman served as mayor from 1883 to 1890. His sons took over the harness shop after he retired. The business closed in 1924, but the building still stands.

Military Avenue is quiet in this modern view looking north. The Baxter Bank building on the northeast corner looks well preserved, but the structure stands empty. On the southeast corner, the Kingrey-Kellum Agency occupies the former Dent's Dry Goods building, and the Baxter Springs school district offices are located in the former drugstore building.

Recalling the annual GAR reunions, Mayor Sam Douthit organized a big birthday party for Baxter Springs in 1926. The event evolved into the annual Frontier Days and Birthday Celebration. This photograph of the parade heading south on Military Avenue past the Marr Grocery Store and Polster Brothers Dry Goods was taken during the 1928 celebration.

The Baxter Springs Heritage Center and Museum at 740 East Street is near the former locations of the springs, Fort Blair, and John Baxter's Inn. The center, operated by the Baxter Springs Historical Society, offers a 20,000-square-foot museum with exhibits on various periods of the city's history, from the days of the Osage Indians through the Route 66 era to the present.

John Polster Jr. and his wife, Christine, brought their family to Baxter Springs in 1866. Polster Brothers Dry Goods and Polster's Drugstore were located in the "Polster Block" on the northwest corner of Ninth Street and Military Avenue. This frame building next door housed the Polster Hotel. John Polster Jr. died in 1880, leaving Christine with six children. She married John A. Sours in 1890.

After a devastating 1893 fire, sons John and Ed Polster relocated the Polster Brothers Dry Goods store a block to the south. A second Polster Block, shown here, was constructed. Polster's Drug Store became Campbell's, and the hotel also occupied the new building. The Polster Brothers Dry Goods Store remained in business until 1939.

Another fire struck the Polster family businesses in 1909, and the third Polster Hotel was constructed of brick. Christine Polster-Sour ran all three incarnations of the hotel from 1873 until she retired in 1926 at the age of 84. At the time, she was the oldest hotel operator in Kansas. This building became the Merry Bales Hotel.

The Diamond service station, operated by William Lloyd Archibald, later occupied the northwest corner of Tenth Street and Military Avenue. The lettering on the side of the hotel next door reflects the change from the Polster Hotel to the Merry Bales. The Merry Bales rated a mention in *A Guide Book to Route 66*, published by Jack Rittenhouse in 1946, but the building is long gone.

By 1946, Diamond service stations had been rebranded as D-X. Lloyd Archibald is at left after his D-X station had joined the trend of stations remodeling in the Streamline style. The station became Sharp's Body Shop, and the building still stands across from the Route 66 Visitors' Center. The other person in the photograph is not identified.

Glenn Pruitt is shown here handing Mickey Mantle the keys to a brand-new Oldsmobile Holiday at Pruitt Motors. The dealership was originally located at 130 East Twelfth Street. Pruitt sold that building to the Lerner Company in 1944 and moved to the Hood Building on the northwest corner of Tenth Street and Military Avenue. The Pruitt home is visible in the background across Ninth Street. Pruitt Motors closed in 1980, but the building still stands.

In 1926, a new Baxter Springs City Hall was completed on the southeast corner of Eleventh Street and Park Avenue during the administration of Mayor Samuel A. Douthit. The corner had once been the site of the First Methodist Church of Baxter Springs. A modern city hall was built at 1445 Military Avenue in 1984, but this building still serves the community as the police station.

The Independent Oil and Gas Company station at Tenth Street and Military Avenue opened on July 7, 1930, and advertised as "one of the district's finest." It was rebranded after Independent merged with Phillips 66 in September 1930. The L-shaped garage addition was constructed in 1942. Phillips sold the station to J.R. Parsons in 1958. (Courtesy of Russell Olsen.)

J.R Parsons sold the station to Phil R. Coulter in 1966. It was later used as office space and then as the home of a dog-grooming business. The Baxter Springs Historical Society purchased the historic station in 2005, and a team of volunteers headed by DeAnn Auman Hill began restoration. The station opened as the Kansas Route 66 Visitors Center on October 13, 2007.

Seen in this view looking south on Military from Tenth Street in the 1950s, Brand's Fashions later became Douthit's Supply. Henry and Louisa Ohlen's Restaurant and Boarding House was next door. It was one of the most popular places in town, in business from 1878 until 1914. The restaurant offered "ice cream and oysters in proper seasons." It was also known as Delmonico's at one time. The building is now gone.

By the 1970s, the former Ohlen's Restaurant housed the Ace Hardware store, where the local Empire District Electric Co. office is today. The Douthit's Plumbing and Electrical Supply location is now a parking lot for Empire Electric. At the time of the photograph, Empire Electric was housed in the darker brick structure next to the hardware store, with the Round-Up Bar next door.

The Marr Grocery Store, operated by the Parham family at the time this image was captured, later became the Round-Up Bar. This building is now occupied by the accounting office of DeAnn Auman Hill. The C.E. Marr chain once operated over 1,000 locations. The Baxter Springs store was No. 12. The Spokane, Washington–based Marr chain merged with Safeway in 1929.

The Fadler Brothers Produce Company was established about 1912 in Pittsburg, Kansas, and added locations in Baxter Springs and Mulberry. This one was just off Military Avenue on Tenth Street behind the Baxter Hotel. When the company reorganized in 1920, a new facility was built in Pittsburg, Kansas, and the company thereafter concentrated its business there.

The Hotel Baxter occupied the northeast corner of Tenth Street and Park Avenue, a block west of Military Avenue. The hotel was damaged by lightning during the 1895 tornado. It became the Occidental Hotel and burned in the 1920s. As of 2016, the corner was the location of the Ministerial Alliance Thrift Shop, housed in a metal warehouse-type building.

The Apostolic Church at Tenth Street and Lincoln Avenue had a neon sign. Charles Fox Parham was the founder of the Apostolic Faith and initially worked out of the old Zellekin Brewery in Baxter Springs. The remodeled building is still the home of the Apostolic Faith Bible College, but the neon sign is gone. (Courtesy of Baxter Springs Heritage Center.)

Another neon cross could be found at the Assembly of God Church, a block off Route 66 at Twelfth Street and Park Avenue. Charles Fox Parham, founder of the Apostolic Faith movement, spent his final years in Baxter Springs and died in 1929. His Apostolic Faith movement merged with other Pentecostal groups to become the Assemblies of God.

Prussian immigrant Julius Bischosberger built a hotel and restaurant on the southeast corner of Tenth Street and Military Avenue in 1868. The hotel and restaurant were torn down in 1900 and this building, which still stands today, was constructed. The Independent Order of Odd Fellows met upstairs, and the building housed the Baxter Springs Post Office until 1911. It later became Baxter Drug.

A fine brick building was constructed in 1870 on the southwest corner of Eleventh Street and Military Avenue to house the Crowell Bank, founded by H.R. Crowell, the second mayor of Baxter Springs. On April 19, 1876, Charlie Pitts and Bill Chadwell of the James-Younger Gang robbed the bank of about $3,000. Jesse James did not take part in the robbery, although local lore often places him there.

The interior of the Crowell Bank was well appointed, but the bank collapsed in 1887. Crowell then established the private Baxter Bank. The building later housed Bill Murphey's Restaurant, then the Sandwich Shop Café, and eventually the Café on the Route, which closed in 2015. The teller cage from the bank can be seen today at the Baxter Springs Heritage Center.

John M. Cooper erected the building at left in 1900 for the Baxter Bank, which later became Baxter National Bank. "The King of the Bank Robbers," Henry Starr, committed one of his 20 career holdups here in 1914. Bill Murphey's Restaurant was located here when it closed in 2008. Read's Drug Store and Harvey's undertakers are visible on the other side of Military Avenue.

Porter Clark's furniture and undertaking business is at right in this view looking north on Military Avenue at Twelfth Street. This was once the site of the Norman Hotel. The building past Clark's is now the Route 66 Soda Fountain, a youth center in a re-created diner with a flashy neon sign. The Gillman Grocery at right center was once the location of the J.P. Opperman Harness and Saddle Shop.

J.C. Penney leased the Clark Furniture and Undertaking building on the northeast corner of Twelfth Street and Military Avenue on January 1, 1927. Penney's closed in 1976, and this building became Jen Smith's Fancy Farmer antiques and boutique in October 2015. Two of four theaters in town, the Ritz and the New Baxter Theaters, were located on the west side of the street.

Sue Gast and Sue Ramage opened Angels on the Route, a popular café and souvenir shop, here in 2008. The building was constructed for John M. Cooper's Dry Goods in 1868. In the 1880s, Cooper moved his business next door to what would become the Ritz Theater. This structure became Reedy's Pharmacy from 1910 until 1958.

The second location of John Cooper's Dry Goods on the northwest corner of Twelfth Street and Military Avenue became the Ritz Theater. It opened on April 30, 1926, showing Paramount's *The Ancient Highway*. From 1957 until 1980, this was the Blue Castle Café, operated by Ralph and Frances Adams. The café closed in 1980, and the building was under renovation in 2016.

In June 1952, Warner Bros., the Ford Motor Company, and the US Highway 66 Association organized a 10-day caravan to dedicate Route 66 as the Will Rogers Highway and promote the movie *The Will Rogers Story*. Will Rogers Jr., Virginia Mayo, and other stars unveiled a plaque at each state line. The caravan also stopped at cinemas along the way, including the New Baxter Theater.

In this view looking south on Military Avenue at Twelfth Street in March 1915, the Chubb Feed Store site is now the location of the American Bank. The Jefferson Highway Garage reflects Military Avenue's designation as "the Jefferson Highway" prior to the creation of the US highway system in 1926. In Baxter Springs, the Jefferson Highway also overlapped with the Ozark Trails Highway, which became Route 66.

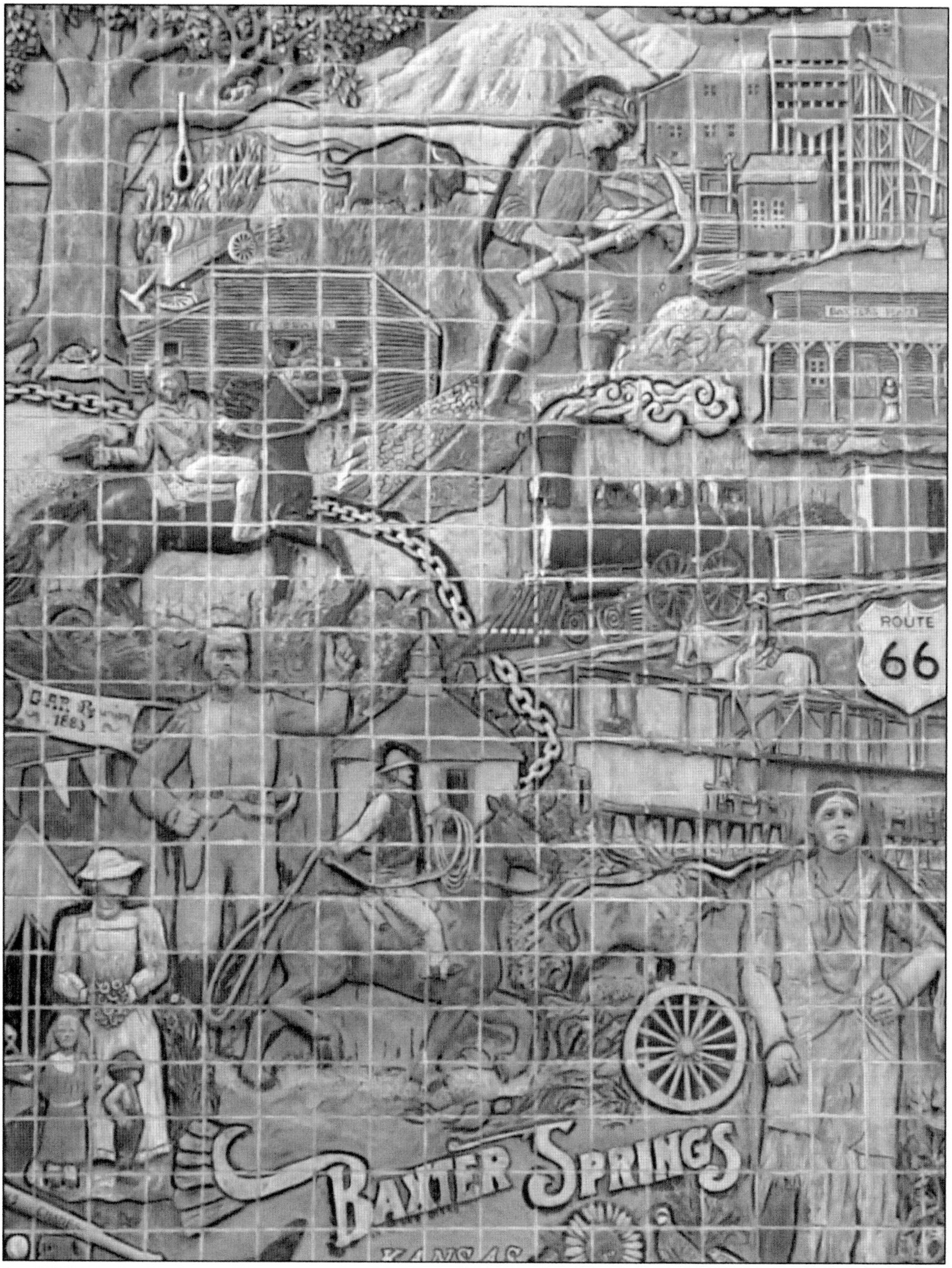

In 1995, Paula Collins of Denton, Texas, created a bas-relief on the side of the American National Bank depicting scenes from the history of Baxter Springs. The scenes include Quantrill's Raid, John Baxter's cabin, and a Route 66 shield. Winding through the design is a depiction of the world's longest wooden chain, carved by Galena resident Jim Porter.

The American National Bank at Twelfth Street and Military Avenue opened in 1917. On September 6, 1933, three members of the Wilbur Underhill Gang robbed the bank when all the police officers were out of town. The firm took over Baxter National Bank in 1952, and the original building and an addition are shown here in 1959. The historic building was replaced in 1976.

The Cunningham Marks Oil Company was on the southeast corner of Twelfth Street and Park Avenue, the eventual site of the American Bank drive-up window. This 1920s photograph shows, from left to right, Ray Kerns, Orville Shipley, and Darrell Jamison. Behind the station was a larger building that contained the oil company offices and a three-bay garage.

Twelfth Street and Park Avenue was once the site of the Empire Hotel, one of the leading hotels in the city. Opened in September 1917, it had 35 rooms, "many of which are equipped with hot and cold running water." From 1925 to 1945, it was owned by Sadie Garrison. Homer and Belle Graber also operated it for many years. The hotel closed in 1973 and was demolished in 1989.

The Lerner Brothers Manufacturing Company was the nation's leading maker of bowling shirts, made under the King Louie label. The factory opened in 1946 at Twelfth and East Streets. The company was sold in 1981 and moved to a new plant near the Walmart. Michael Lerner bought the firm in 2015, keeping jobs in Baxter Springs. The old plant still stands.

This Phillips 66 station was one of three in Baxter Springs during the Route 66 era and was located on the northeast corner of Twelfth and East Streets. It was operated by Herbert L. Weaver from the early 1960s until 1972. As of 2016, the site was occupied by the Fastrip convenience store and station.

The Kenneth Schurman Funeral Home was once the residence of James Walter Grantham and his wife, Pearl. In 1932, the Granthams moved into the home at the old Joplin Country Club that later became the Spring River Inn. Grantham owned mining interests, a music store, and a couple of theaters. The former funeral home is now the Derfelt Baxter Springs Chapel.

At the time of this 1924 photograph, the H.W. Price Motor Company was located on Military Avenue between Twelfth and Thirteenth Streets. The business opened in September 1922 as a Chevrolet agency. From left to right, Merle Winters, Ted Hartley (who later opened a Buick dealership), Joe Standifer, Archie Brock, and Raymond Williams pose in front of several Chevys.

A sign outside KMT Water Jet Systems boasts "the Birthplace of Water Jet Cutting." McCartney Manufacturing started out in 1947 at the former Cunningham Marks Oil Company, shown here in 1950. It moved a few blocks to the west in 1954. In 1963, Joe McCartney sold to Ingersoll-Rand, now KMT. Water jets under intense pressure can cut through nearly any object.

The Keeton Oil Company was located on the northwest corner of Thirteenth Street and Military Avenue. Note the 66 highway shield at left of photograph and the electric car tracks in the foreground running down the center of Military Avenue. This structure is long gone. The site is now a small park area on the American Bank block.

Maurice and Mary Byrd opened Byrd's Drive-In at 1401 Military Avenue after World War II. Their ads featured catchy slogans such as, "If you can't stop, wave," and "Let the Byrds feed you." In 1954, the Byrds moved out west but eventually retired to Cassville, Missouri. The drive-in closed in the mid-1960s, and the Ford dealer across the street used it for a used car lot.

This photograph of the Baxter Springs Texaco service station was taken around 1950. The station was located at Fourteenth Street and Military Avenue. The Texaco stations of the era, painted white with green streamline stripes, were designed by Walter Dorwin Teague, who also designed the Kodak Brownie camera. Star Lube Auto Express Care now occupies this corner.

The Dairy Queen in Baxter Springs opened in 1947, the only franchised restaurant in town at the time. It was still one of the only walk-up Dairy Queens remaining in the United States when Bob and Jean Jenkins sold it to Darren Abbott in 1991. The building was replaced that year, and it became the Mother Road Steak House and Grill in 1999.

Many residents remember swimming lessons and fun at the Baxter Springs Municipal Pool on East Sixteenth Street, just off Military Avenue. This photograph, taken in 1956, shows students displaying their newfound swimming skills for parents and family members. The Central Elementary School is in the background.

With its carhops and jukebox, the C & S Drive In was a typical teen hangout. Cliff Congdon and Fred Sweet opened it in the 1950s at Eighteenth Street and Military Avenue and then sold to Pete and Sybil McGregor, who constructed a new building in the 1960s. The McGregors later returned and ran it until the 1980s. This painting of the drive-in was done in 1967 by Jim Skaggs.

Corbin Shouse Sr. (left) and Fred Shouse pose with their oil supplier Ray Parsons (center) outside their station in 1935. The Shouse Service Station was located at Nineteenth Street and Military Avenue. The station was remodeled, and a canopy was added in the 1950s. It has since housed a series of businesses and, as of 2016, was occupied by B and D Tire.

Orville and Phyliss Mehaffy acted and sang with the "Toby and Susie Traveling Show" before purchasing the Capistrano Motel in 1954. They operated the 16-unit motel at 2200 South Military until 1977. Harry and Nell Miller bought the Capistrano and operated it until 1988, when it was demolished. The site is now home to Cowtown Liquors.

Ted Hartley's Buick dealership, located in the 2200 block of South Military Avenue, is shown in this 1962 photograph. The business was just south of the Capistrano Motel. After the dealership closed, the building also housed the Sugar Bear Club, Cowtown Restaurant, and Video Mart. The building stands empty as of 2015.

Fred Lammers sold ice, bait, film, souvenirs, and just about anything else at the Ice House. The family lived in a house next door, and they had a liquor store to the north. Bob Myers took over the liquor store about 1980 and added a miniature golf course in the back. At that time, John Burrows took over the bait shop. The building still stands as of 2016.

Members of the seven-man Baxter Springs Police Department pose in 1957 with their Ford police cruiser. Baxter Springs' finest are, from left to right, Chief Percy Brown, Desk Sgt. Edward Anderson, Patrolman Sam Downes, Patrolman Roy Wright, Asst. Chief Charles Davis, Patrolman Willis Clark, and Patrolman Taylor Moore.

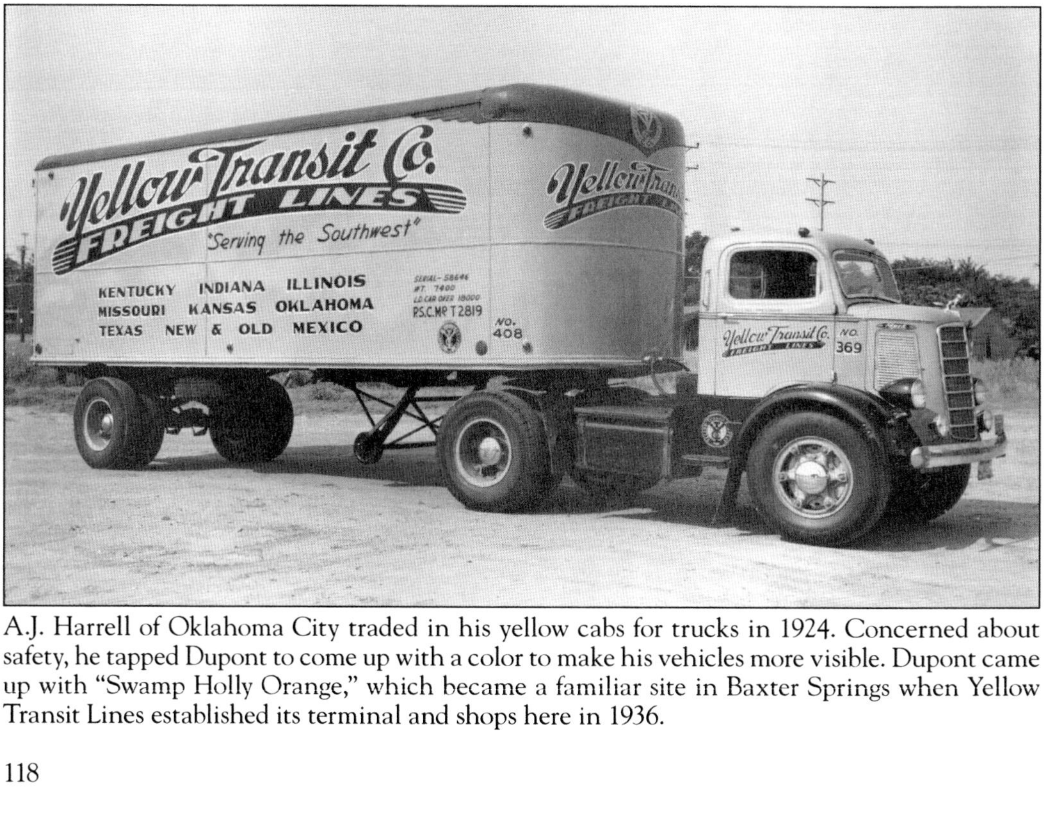

A.J. Harrell of Oklahoma City traded in his yellow cabs for trucks in 1924. Concerned about safety, he tapped Dupont to come up with a color to make his vehicles more visible. Dupont came up with "Swamp Holly Orange," which became a familiar site in Baxter Springs when Yellow Transit Lines established its terminal and shops here in 1936.

At one time, there were five national truck lines operating out of Baxter Springs. Yellow Transit, which became Yellow Freight in 1968, employed 150 people and was moving 150 trucks through town each day. The terminal on Twelfth Street was abandoned in the 1970s and a larger facility was built on Powell Road, south of town. The firm is now known as YRC Freight.

Before a bridge over the Spring River east of Baxter Springs opened in the 1880s, operators of a cable ferry would charge immigrants double the usual toll. The wooden structure at the dam was next to the Baxter Springs Flouring Mill, just out of view on the west side of the river. Part of this bridge collapsed in 1926 under the weight of two Atlas Powder Company trucks loaded with dynamite for the mines. The road here became Route 166 that same year.

The second Spring River Bridge on Route 166 was 525 feet long, constructed in 1943, and torn down in 1989 for a generic concrete deck bridge. Route 166 is one of the two Route 66 spurs remaining as US highways, since Route 666 was renumbered in 2003. The riverbank is now a popular spot for camping and fishing, but it was once used as a trash dump.

This 1917 bridge carried the Southwest Missouri Electric Railway over the Spring River, the island, and a smaller branch to the east. The closed spandrel concrete arch bridge is about 1,400 feet long. Abandoned since the 1930s, it still stands, due largely to preservation efforts in the 1990s led by Phyllis Abbott.

Original Route 66 made an S-curve on the south side of Baxter Springs in front of the Baxter Modern Cabins. Locals say a couple having an affair was killed by a gas leak in one of the cabins, and the two were found in each other's arms. The cabins closed in 1965. Walmart was built on the site, between old Route 66 and the new road.

Baxter Springs is the hometown of former Walmart CEO Leo Scott, but that did not stop the company from closing one of its last original format stores on April 28, 2015, after over 30 years in business. Company officials said store No. 208 was obsolete because it did not have a full-fledged grocery department. The Baxter IGA shown in this image was replaced by a Dollar General.

Mary's Café was next to the Port of Entry near the Kansas-Oklahoma line from 1952 until 1954. Bill and Wanda Murphey later operated it as the Ranch House Restaurant. In the early 1950s, a tornado damaged the restaurant and killed two residents in a nearby home. The café was torn down in 1957, and Danny's Tire is located here now.

The Twilite Drive-In, one mile south of Baxter Springs on Route 66, opened on June 11, 1953, with a showing of *The Magic Carpet*, starring Lucille Ball and John Agar. The drive-in included a playground for the children and a modern concession stand. In May 1978, a severe storm destroyed most of the screen, and the Twilite never reopened. A few ruins remain today.

The state lines of Missouri, Kansas, and Oklahoma meet about seven miles east of Baxter Springs on a dead-end road just off Routes 166 and 400 and the driveway to the Downstream Casino. The northern boundary line of Oklahoma was established in 1857 by an 800-member expedition that took six months. The Youth Work Administration constructed a rock monument here in 1938.

More recent surveys found that the actual point where the three borders of Kansas, Oklahoma, and Missouri meet is about 50 feet southeast of the original monument. A flat marker was installed here in 2004 by the Missouri Department of Natural Resources, and it is possible to stand in three states at the same time.

This view looks back into Kansas from the Oklahoma state line during the 1940s. Just over one-half mile to the north, a right turn on Thirtieth Street leads to the original section of Route 66 behind the closed Walmart. It is marked by Route 66 shields painted on the pavement. The old route merges onto Roberts Road, rejoins Route 69, and becomes Military Avenue heading into Baxter Springs.

Beneath one of the rare Kansas Route 66 shields, a sign warns that tractors with lugged wheels are prohibited. Old tractors used steel wheels with lugs, or spikes, which improved traction in the fields, but those intimidating-looking wheels chewed up the road surface. Farmers had to either travel in the ditch alongside the road or switch to rubber tires.

Twilight for Route 66 in Kansas came on June 28, 1957, with the opening of the Will Rogers Turnpike in Oklahoma. In 1961, the section of Interstate 44 between Joplin and the Will Rogers Turnpike was completed, and Kansas became the only Route 66 state to be completely bypassed. After decertification in 1985, the highway from Oklahoma to Riverton became Route 69A and the route from Riverton to the Missouri Line became KS 66.

The unidentified traveler met at the beginning of this journey also took time to pose for a photograph at the Kansas-Oklahoma state line. Ahead is Oklahoma, the home of Will Rogers and Cyrus Avery, as well as memories of the desperate Dust Bowl days. Oklahoma can boast more miles of Route 66 remaining than any other state.

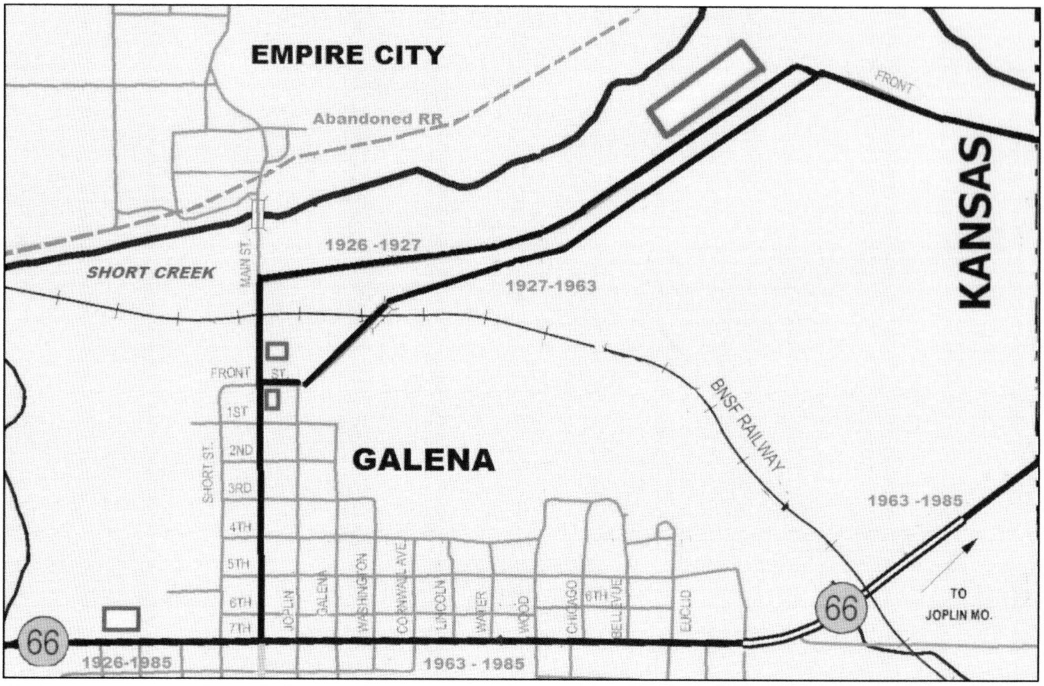

Galena embraced three different alignments of Route 66 into the city. The two earlier alignments, 1926–1927 and 1927–1963, brought motorists into Galena from the north. The second of these, the 1927–1963 alignment, today brings tourists into town at the intersection of Front and Main Streets, where popular attractions Cars on the Route and the Murder Bordello are located. Seventh Street carried the 1963–1985 alignment. (Kansas Department of Transportation.)

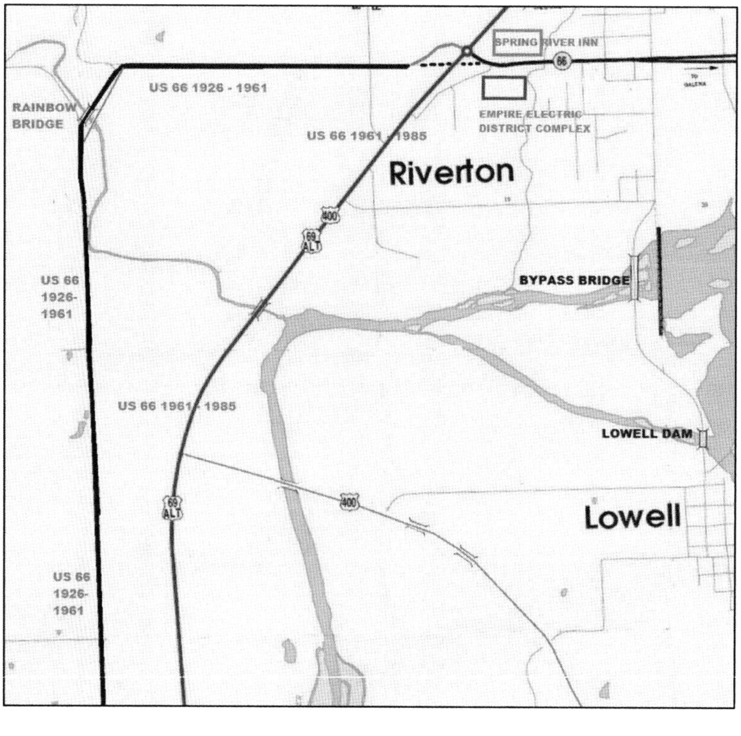

From Galena, the 1926–1961 alignment of Route 66 first took motorists straight west through Riverton. The highway then turned southwest to cross Brush Creek over a Marsh arch bridge. Named for its designer, James Marsh, this is the only remaining one of three such bridges on Kansas Route 66. From the bridge, this alignment went straight south to Baxter Springs. A 1961–1985 alignment curved toward Baxter Springs. (Kansas Department of Transportation.)

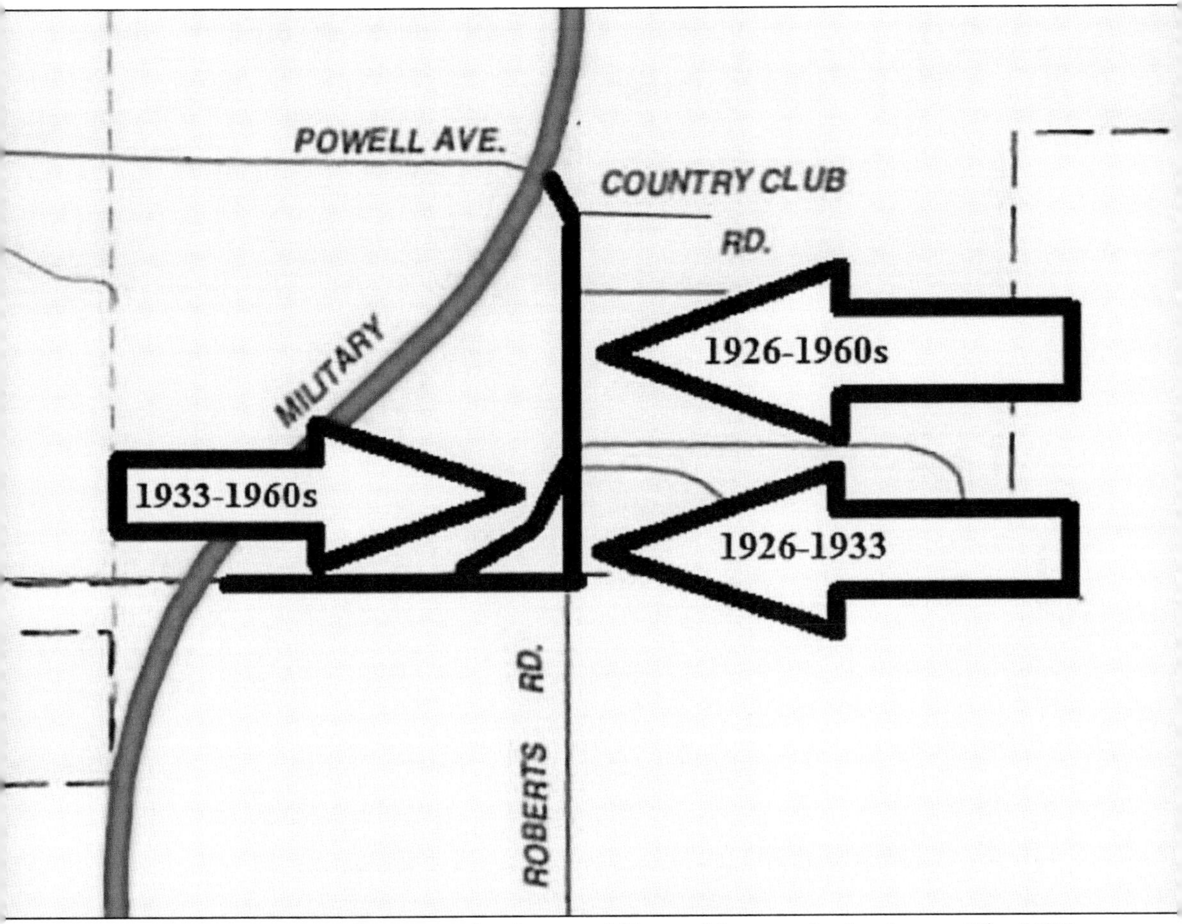

South of Baxter Springs, a short stretch of original Route 66 is worth the detour. The 1926 alignment dropped south along Roberts Road and made a sharp turn west on West Thirtieth Street to rejoin Military Avenue. The curve was straightened in 1933 and again in the 1960s with a new alignment of Military Avenue. (Kansas Department of Transportation.)

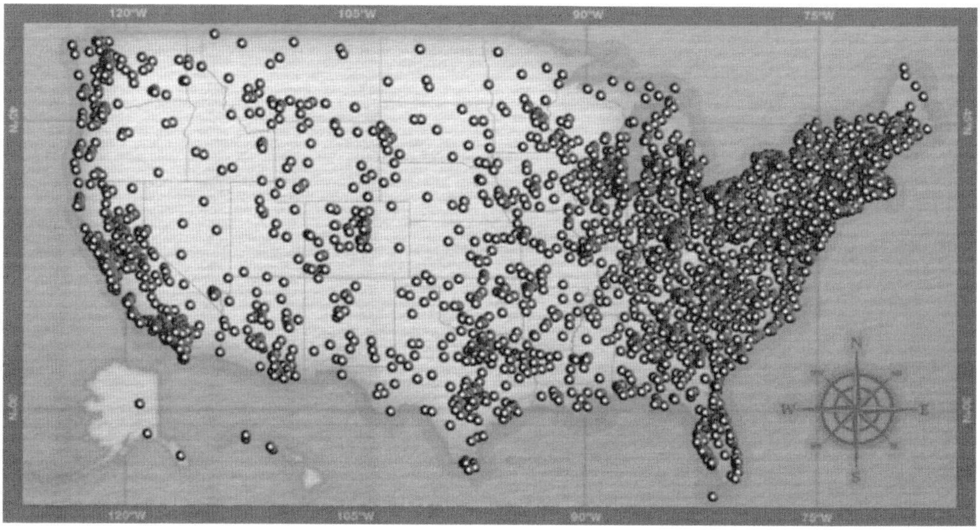